Options Trading for Beginners

Learn Strategies from the Experts on how to Day Trade Options for a Living!

David Hewitt & Andrew Peter

Table of Contents

Introduction

There is no doubt that the global economy is always experiencing alteration from time to time. The increase in the world population is gradually affecting the availability of jobs, and with millions of people not getting access to a collar job, online trading, cryptocurrencies, and options trading are some of the leading business ventures that people now show interest in. However, as the number of people who are interested in options trading keeps increasing, we have discovered that the ignorance rate is expanding. There is no other greatest limiting factor to success in whatever step you take in life than ignorance. And this truth applies to option trading. If you want to get the best result, then you've got to learn from experts who have done it before, who are doing it and don't plan to stop at it.

Options trading is an opportunity for anyone who wishes to earn without much stress, but this is only possible if you have a clear knowledge about it. With over four decades of existence, options trading recently started gathering waves. Do you know why? Many people believe it is hard and sophisticated. As a result of this belief, many investors didn't want to invest in it. However, options trading is not difficult. You only need to learn about it to get the excellent result you seek. Without the right knowledge, you risk the possibility of losing your investment. If all you pay attention to is the use of words, such as *risky* or *dangerous* by the media, you will most definitely not consider options trading.

Just before you make your conclusion on a baseless misconception by others, just note that engaging in options trading gives you access to an increased cost-efficiency. It is not as risky as equities, you have access to several strategic alternatives, and with the right tools and knowledge, options trading promises potential high percentage returns; and most importantly, it is a reliable means of making passive income. With the knowledge in this book, you are set to learn the strategies to improve your portfolio.

This book is a guide you need to gain access to the necessary information you must have before you venture into the options trading world. We have provided information on how options trading works, the very strategies you need to succeed at it, how to

5

understand when to trade and when you should not trade, handing technical analysis, and building your wealth with risk management. We will not promise you that there are no challenges you will face while options trading, but we can assure you that with this book, you will be equipped to face the challenges. This guide is a compendium of answers to every possible question you may have about options trading.

The next investment move you need to make to start experiencing the financial freedom lifestyle you seek is to begin options trading now. It is an opportunity that is best grasped now. A good time for you to start options trading is yesterday, and the best time is now. Learn and digest the strategies and tips in this book and begin on a journey to achieve financial freedom in no time!

Chapter One: Unveiling Options

In the world of possibilities that we live in, taking hold of options trading is a great way to grasp one of the opportunities that the world really has to offer. Options trading makes it easy and possible for your money to work for you while you follow your other passions. With your money constantly at work, it is so easy for you to achieve the financial freedom and success you seek. So, what is options trading, and how does it work?

What is an Option?

An option is a contract that offers an investor the right to purchase or sell a security at a specific price with an agreement for a certain period. When you trade options, you are trading different securities such as ETFs, indices, equities, and many more. Options enjoy their value from their underlying assets, and this is why they are often referred to as *derivatives.* There is an options market where investors meet to buy and sell options. The contracts that are traded on the market are based on the securities hip in a company. Unlike a stock that gives you an ownership right of a company, option buying and selling gives you the ability to trade the obligation or potential to buy and sell the underlying stock of a company. If you own an option, you are not entitled to any dividend payments.

When you buy or sell options, you have the right to exercise the option at any period during the contract lifetime. What this means is that you don't have to exercise buying and selling of an option at the buy and sell point. This is why options are derivative securities. Being derivatives means they derive their price from another item or product, which will be the value of assets, such as securities and the market. In a way, the derivative nature of options makes them less risky than stocks. But to make this work for you, you've got to understand how to use options correctly.

As an investor, how do you use options? It is simple. When you buy options, you are gambling on the available stocks to either go up or down or, let me say; you are hedging a trading position in the market. So, the agreed rate you pay for the underlying asset through the option is the *strike price*. But the fee you pay for buying the option is *premium*. During the process of considering and stating the *strike price*, what you do is to gamble that the price of a particular asset which may be a stock, ETFs, etc., will go up or down. And *premium* is the payment you make for the bet, and *a premium* will is always a percentage of the asset's value.

Types of Options

There are two fundamental types of options—call option and put option. These two forms are responsible for offering an investor the right, but not the obligation, to either sell or buy securities. As a beginner who is making an effort to learn options trading, you've got to understand these two forms.

Call Options

Call options are the right an investor has to buy a specific amount of security or financial products at an agreed price over a period of time. In other words, it gives a holder, who is a buyer, to buy the stock. Investors put their money in a call option when they want the security or stock to increase in price. This is how they are able to make a profit off their contract by using their right to purchase the stocks or securities. Remember, I mentioned *premium earlier*. So, the *premium* is the cost you use to buy the contract that will give you the right to eventually buy the security or stock when the time reaches. *The premium* of a call option works like a downpayment you make on security, asset, or stock.

During the purchase of a call option, the seller agrees with you on a specific amount—*strike price*, and you will have the option to buy the asset at an already agreed price, and the price doesn't change until the expiration of the contract. The call option helps you plan for the future. By paying for the contract that will expire later, you are buying an asset at an already decided price, and the price of the asset, security, or stock will not rise even if the price of the asset rises in the market. When you have a lower *strike price* for a call option, you have got a high intrinsic value.

Example of Call Option

We would love to give you a more practical example to show you what the call option really means. Let's use real estate as an example. Mr. A is a potential homeowner, and he sees a development in the desired area, but Mr. A is only willing to exercise the right to own a home in the area when a certain level of development has been achieved. A call option will make this possible for Mr. A. How? If the developer is willing to sell a call option to him. Let's say The developer is willing to sell the home at $500,000 to Mr. A, in the next two years, in the area; the developer will ask Mr. A to buy a call option of, let's say, $50,000. This price is the premium that Mr. A is paying for the *striking price* of $500,000. The $50,000 is non-refundable, and it is a down payment that Mr. A makes to the developer with the expectation that he will buy the asset between now when the contract starts and the next two years when the contract expires.

If two years come, and the area has developed as projected by Mr. A, he can go ahead and pay for the home at $500,000 regardless of the present value of the home, which may be between $700,000 and $900,000. But since he has made a downpayment, the call option gives him the right to it at the agreed price. There is, however, a possible unwanted situation if, for instance, the development approval of the area failed to work out within the space of three years, which is now a year after the expiration of the contract, Mr. A will have to buy the home at the current market price because the call option has expired and in both cases, the developer keeps the *premium:$50,000.*

Put Options

A put option occurs the other way round. It gives an investor the right to sell securities. So, with the put option, you have the right to sell a specific amount of shares, securities, or assets over a certain period. The seller only has the right but not the obligation to sell, and the selling must be done within the contract's expiration date. Strike price and premium also work for put options. The basic difference is that when you buy the put option, you are most likely expecting a fall in the price of the asset. Most importantly, the higher the stake price for a put option, the higher the intrinsic value that the put option has.

Example of a Put Option

For a put option, let's use the stock as an example. A put option works like insurance to protect against risk or loss. So, let's say Mr. A wants to protect his stocks, having seen traces of a possible bear market insight and doesn't want to lose more than 5% of his investments. If the stock is presently trading at $1,250, Mr. A can buy a put option that will give him the right to sell the stocks at $1,000 within the next year. Let's say in the next three months; the market eventually crashes by 40%; Mr. A will make up for his loss by selling his stock at $1,000 when it is trading at $750. If the market doesn't fall within the period, the only loss Mr. A incurs is the premium.

Whether you buy a call or put option, the result is usually with the aim of increasing your money. If you've got the right knowledge to go about it, you would be amazed at how well you would succeed and make tremendous profits.

Why You Should Trade Options

If you don't know the reason you should engage in options trading, we will show you three basic reasons.

Make more money: Who doesn't want to make more money? Well, there is none. We are all working tirelessly every day to achieve our financial goals and live life as we want it. With options trading, you can sell puts or write calls on your shares or assets to make more money while you still have it. In a situation where the stock, for instance, moves above the strike price, by the end of the contract, you may have to buy or sell the stock. Regardless, you have the option premiums as the income you earn.

It helps to hedge risks: With options, you can set certain risk parameters around your securities and assets. Options help you, like insurance, to protect your investments and reduce risks if you are able to use them well. For example, rather than placing a stop-loss order on your stock, you may buy put options to create downside protection for the stock.

It gives room for Speculation: If you capitalize on options, you will be able to leverage and make a bet on moves in whatever direction, whether up, down, or sideways. It gives you access to greater gains (and loses at times.) You don't need a large capital to make high profits with options trading.

Just as it is with every other investment, options trading comes with its risks and benefits. If you are equipped with the basic knowledge and information about how it works, you will find it easy to succeed at putting your resource in options trading. Before we take you deeper into the cores and methods of options trading, let's take a quick tour around some basic terminology you need to familiarize yourself with.

Option Trading Language

Option trading occurs in a wide market, and it involves a wide range of features and strategies. As a result, there are lots of terms that traders use while engaging in options trading. We will not be able to look at all of these terms, but we will definitely look at the basic ones you need to know as a beginner, and as you proceed into the book and trade, you will get to learn more.

Call/call option: It is an option contract that allows you to have the right to buy an asset or security at an agreed price within a certain timeframe.

Put/ put option: It gives you the right to sell assets or securities at a particular point in time over a certain period.

Expiration date: This is the day the option contract becomes inactive. The date depends on the agreement between the seller and buyer.

Break-Even Point: This refers to the price range of underlying assets with no profits or losses.

Bull market: It is used to express that the market, in general, is experiencing growth.

Strike price/ exercise price: It is the price at which you can either buy or sell an asset if you decide to exercise the option.

Premium: It is the price for an option. Premium is made up of intrinsic value and time value.

Intrinsic value: It is the value of the option as a result of the difference between the current market price of a stock and the strike price of the option.

Time value: This is the value of an option as a result of the length of the contract expiration date.

Bear Market: This is used when the market, in general, experiences a decline.

Last: This is the price that was paid or received at the last transaction when the option was traded.

In the money: It is used to express the worth of an option in terms of its intrinsic value. So, this expression shows that the relationship between the asset price in the open market and the strike price favors the contract owner.

Out of the Money: This expression is used to show that there is no financial benefit to exercising the option. So, if the asset price is lower than the strike price, the call option is out of the money. And when the asset price is higher than the strike price, the put option is out of the money.

At the Money: It shows that the asset or stock price is almost equal to the strike price.

Bid: Bid is the amount a buyer has decided to pay for an option. The bid is the premium a seller receives.

Ask: Ask is the amount a seller is willing to receive for an option.

Bullish: It is an expectation that an option, assets, share, or securities will experience an increase in price.

Volume: It is the number of contracts that are traded in a day.

Open interest: This is the amount of options contracts that are in play.

Volatility: It is used to express the measurement of the rate at which an asset price rises and falls every day.

Holder: Rather than the term buyer or seller, options trading has its terms. A holder is an investor who pays for an option to buy an asset or stock within the purview of an agreed contract. A call holder buys an asset, while a put holder sells it.

Writer: The writer refers to the investor who is selling the contract. So, the premium goes to the writer from the holder.

The holder and writer are exposed to risk on a different level. Holders only buy the right to either buy or sell an asset or share. They are not under compulsion to do any. So a holder can decide to exercise the option (which means to buy) or just walk away if they meet with an out-of-the-money situation. The only thing they lose is their premium and the trade commission. However, writers have more to lose. In a situation where the holder is ready to exercise an option, the writer must fulfill the order and sell the asset or share to the holder regardless of the present market value of the option. As a beginner, it is best to start your options trading as a holder to maximize your profit and learn before you advance. Take your time to have a clear understanding of the basics of options trading. We have got awesome knowledge to divulge.

Chapter Two: Risk and Rewards—Your Playground

Risk is an essential part of every investment, and if you want to go into options trading, you must be ready to face the risks that come with it. Risks shouldn't stop you from investing. You need to be more focused and have a clear-cut plan that you will use to deal with it in order to maximize profits. In general, risks mean the probability of losing money in an investment. Options trading has a high level of risk because there is a possibility of a leveraged loss of trading capital as a result of the leveraged nature of stock options. Ignorance about the risks associated with options trading has been a leading reason many people believe it is a difficult investment to go into. With the right level of information, you will succeed in your training. Let's take you through some pertinent risks that come with options trading.

Primary Risks

Possible Losses

The greatest strength of options trading is the benefit it offers, in that, you can utilize leverage to increase your capital strength. It works in a way that if you purchase a call option of a company's stock that is worth $2,000, there is a probability that you could make so much profit. In case the stock increases, all you've got to do is to invest the $2,000 into the stock. This is the profit it offers, and in this strength lies one of its risks. In a situation where the stock falls or fails to rise but stays still, you will lose your call options and the $2,000. If you had spent $2,000 to buy the stock, you would lose the money only.

The main risk is that the options you buy may expire worthlessly, and this will make you lose all you've invested in the contracts. The same loss is applicable to you if you are writing options. This often happens when the underlying security moves unexpectedly in price. You can deal with this risk by using stop loss orders or by creating spreads.

The Advancement of Options Trading.

Naturally, options trading is a complex form of investment, and this makes it risky. It is not an investment portfolio that anyone will just dabble into. You've got to learn it from the basics to the advanced levels. The truth is, it is quite easy to know the basics, but there are certain aspects and strategies that are hard to use because of their complexities. As a beginner, you may find it hard to understand some of the complex methods. If you are not careful, you are bound to make huge mistakes. But there is also good news about this. Learning about it and the various complex strategies will do the magic.

Time Decay

Time decay is an inevitable risk that comes with option trading. For every option, there is a time value attached to it. The length of the expiration of the contract, the higher the time value. So, when you have options, know that they are losing value as time keeps counting. At times, they may not go down in value, but with time decay, the value of your options may be negatively impacted.

Option is liquid

Now, you can see options being traded by more and more people. This is because investors are getting involved by the day. And with the liquidity state of some options, issues tend to arise. Since there are various forms of options, you are likely to find the options that interest you in low quantity. And this will make it difficult for you to trade because you are most likely going to find it hard to make the required trades at the best prices.

The cost incurred in Trading options

Another risk you are likely to face is in the aspect of the options contract prices. These prices are often quoted on the exchanges, and they go with bid prices and ask prices. The price you get for writing options is the bid price, while the price you pay for buying options is the asking price. Usually, the asking price is higher than the bid price, and there is a difference between the two prices called the bid-ask spread. It is the indirect cost of trading options. The rate of the costs is dependent on how big the spread is. If there is no liquidity, the spreads will be bigger, and this speaks to a high level of risk.

Just like every other form of investment, options trading comes with specific risks. These risks are calculated and can therefore be managed with the right plans and procedures in place. Knowledge is the key you need to trade and minimize the risks you tend to face.

Managing Your Risks

The risks attached to options trading can be managed with the right steps and actions. Let's share some practical ways you can go about this:

Engage in position minimizing: Position minimizing is an effective step to reduce risk and save yourself a lot of money. But how does it work? Whenever you purchase options, you tend to lose the amount you spend to buy the option contract if the option expires without increasing in worth. But with position minimizing, you will deal with this. Position minimizing means you should not spend more than 1% to 2% of your investment capital. So, if your option trading account is made up of $100,000, make sure that the highest option trade you go for is $1,000.

Utilize Fix loss option: Fix loss option comes in handy when you need to cap the total amount of what you lose if any factors work against your short option. It is better to purchase your hedge at the location of the rate you plan to cap your losses at.

Set up a stop loss: Your risk will be in the stock if you sell a covered call. What you need at this point is to set up a stop loss for the position of your stock in places where you need to cut your losses short. And you should buy in order to cover your short call.

You can use a stop loss if you sell a married put. This is because your risk is in the short stock. So, set up a stop loss for the position of your short stock where you will cut your losses short and purchase to close your short put option and cover your short stock.

Avoid putting on option plays that have open risk or those that you cannot define their risks. Exposing yourself to unlimited risk options and those that are uncapped portends a high level of risks. On the negative side, you are likely to lose a lot. So, it is best that you have an exit strategy each time you sell options contracts. You can use option hedges because they work as insurance, and they tend to pay for themselves over a long period of time.

Preparing for risk is your duty as an investor. You cannot do without facing the possibility of losing some amount. But you can protect your money by putting in the hard work. One of the most effective skills you need to manage risk is being able to analyze the options trading market. With these skills, you will be amazed at how well you will excel.

Chapter Three: Becoming a Market Analyst

Understanding how the options trading market works is needed for you to be an effective options trader. The options market is used to explain the total activities of buying and selling of options done globally and in regions. There is a close tie between the option trading market and the stock market. The reason is that stocks are commonly traded forms of options. Also, you have access to options based on some other instrument of finances, which include indices, futures, commodities, and currencies. The options market works on volatility. Your ability to work with this in the market will guide you as you further make decisions on the best strategies to use and those to abandon.

Market Volatility

The options market often runs on the volatility of prices. Volatility refers to the metric of how to price changes in the options market within a period of time. In a situation where market volatility is high, the premium pay for options will be highly expensive, and when the volatility is low, the premiums are very cheap. Volatility is shown in the level of variability that is present in the price change of financial security, such as a stock or index. The level of the variability shows the rate of volatility. As much as the market can be volatile, there can also be a nonvolatile market. A nonvolatile market is one where there is no change in prices at all, and when changes try to occur, it comes slowly.

In options marketing, volatile trading is possible, and it refers to trading the volatility of a financial instrument instead of trading the original price. When you trade on volatility, you will not be concerned about how the prices move or the direction the prices go. You are only concerned with the movement of the price of the instrument in the future. With options, you can adequately trade on volatility. This is why the predicted future volatility of the underlying instrument of an option is the bedrock of the option's value. If you trade options that are on instruments that come with high levels of future volatility, you have got a valuable option. The expected future volatility value determines the value of the options.

Generally, financial instruments such as stocks, indexes, and more, that are more volatile, often experience changes in their prices. For options, the practical value, which is the extrinsic value, rises or falls based on the expected volatility.

Volatility is an essential element of every financial market. The reason is that lack of volatility will bring about a lack of profit potential in the markets. Volatility is what both investors and traders thrive on. As a beginner, understand that you cannot make any breaks without dealing with volatility. As much as volatility increases the risks that come with options trading, it, at the same time, serves as the basis upon which you can reap good returns from your investment if used well.

There are two types of volatility in the options market.

Historical Volatility

This form of volatility is used to measure the past volatile rate of the market. Historical volatility is often based on a specific period in the past, which may be a year, months, or weeks. The least and standard period of time used for historical calculation volatility is 20 days. The reason is that options trading only occurs twenty days a month. What historical volatility does is annualize the standard deviation of the changes that occurred in price, showing it as a percentage.

Historical volatility is often carried out by determining the average deviation from the average price of a certain financial instrument in a specific period. Standard deviation is the commonest way to calculate historical volatility, and there are other methods you can use. The security risk is dependent on how high the historical volatility value is, and the same rule works for it when it brings good returns. Investors don't use historical volatility for the purpose of measuring the likelihood of losing, but it can be used to do so. It is usually used to measure the distance a security price has from its mean value. If the market is trending, historical volatility helps to measure the distance between the traded prices and the central average, or moving average price. With this, a trending market will experience low volatility even as the prices change over time.

Implied Volatility

This is the second type of volatility. And it refers to the opinion of the market on the volatility of the underlying security of an option. The volatility is determined by certain information, which includes the price of the underlying security (stock, index, futures, etc.), the option's market price, the interest rate, the option's strike price, the option's expiration date, and the dividends. All of these sets of information are determined using different theoretical option pricing models, which include the black Scholes models.

Unlike historical volatility that measures the changes experienced in the past market and the result obtained, implied volatility gives investors the opportunity to predict the future moves, demand, supply and help them employ the predictions in price options contracts. Implied volatility is represented with the *sigma symbol* (σ). At times, it is considered to be a proxy of market risk, and it is expressed commonly through the use of percentages and standard deviations over a certain time horizon. Whenever the implied volatility is applied to the stock market, it goes up in bearish markets, at the point when investors expect equity prices to fall over time. However, it decreases when the market is bullish, and the investors expect the prices to come up over time. For every investor, bearish markets are risky and undesirable. Note that, with implied volatility, you will not gain access to the direction in which the change in price will take. While high volatility shows that there is a large swing in price, it doesn't show whether the price swings up, down, very high, very low, or keeps fluctuating between the two directions. When the volatility is low, it only shows that the price will not likely make unpredictable changes.

Options and Implied Volatility

The pricing of options is dependent on so many factors, of which implied volatility is an essential one. Implied volatility gives an approximate value of the future of an option by taking the current value of the option into consideration. As a result, an investor will pay high premiums for options that have high implied value otherwise for options with low implied volatility. One crucial thing you must note is that implied volatility works on probability. It gives just an estimate of future prices and not an indication of the prices. The truth is, there is no absolute guarantee that the price of the option will follow the predicted pattern. Nonetheless, it offers a handsome help during the consideration for an investment to know the decisions of other investors with options trading, and in a way, since it is correlated with the opinion of the market, it affects options pricing.

Calculating Volatility

As a trader or an investor, you can calculate volatility. To do this, you will have to use variance and standard deviation. The standard deviation is the traditional method of carrying out this measurement. It measures the distance between the current price and the option's mean or moving average. The standard deviation refers to the square root of the variance.

Let's quickly take a glance at this example to have a clear picture of what it means.

Assuming you have a monthly stock with the closing prices of $1 all through $10. What this means is that, for ten months, you have closing prices of your stock with a $1 increase: In the first month, you have $1, second month, you get $2, month 3, you get $3, month 4, you get $4 until you reach $10. You can calculate the variance of this stock by using these steps below:

Start by identifying the mean of the data set: What this means is that you will add each value and divide it by the number of the value.

So, you will add $1 to $2 to $3 to $4 until you get to $10. With this, you will have $. Then, you will divide it by $10 since you have got 10 numbers in your data set. So, you will have a mean or an average price of $5.50.

Do the calculation of the differences that exist between every data value and the mean or average price: This calculation is what is referred to as deviation. So, you will calculate this way:

Take $10 -$5.50 = $4.50

Take $9 - $5.50 = $3.50

Take $8 - $5.50 = $2.50

You will keep doing this until you reach the first data value of $1. Note that you will get negative numbers, and it is fine because you need all of the values. once you are done with these steps for each of the values, do the following:

Square each of the deviations, and you will easily do away with the negative values.

Now, add all the squared deviations, and in the example above, you will get 82.5.

Then, divide the total of all the squared deviations, which is 82.5, by the number of data values (10 in this example.) You will get $8.25 as the variance, and then you will take the square root of this value to get the standard deviation. The Standard deviation then is $2.87.

With this calculation, you have measured the risk and expressed how values can be spread out around the mean or average price. Traders and investors will know the possible distance the price can go from the average price. You can check the table below for the input of the example above.

	A	B	C	D	E	F
1	Price	Mean	Deviation	Deviation Squared	Variance	Standard Deviation
2	1	5.5	-4.5	20.25		
3	2	5.5	-3.5	12.25		
4	3	5.5	-2.5	6.25		
5	4	5.5	-1.5	2.25		
6	5	5.5	-0.5	0.25		
7	6	5.5	0.5	0.25		
8	7	5.5	1.5	2.25		
9	8	5.5	2.5	6.25		
10	9	5.5	3.5	12.25		
11	10	5.5	4.5	20.25		
12	55			82.5	8.25	2.872281323

(investopedia.com)

Trading Volatility

As mentioned earlier, investors and traders who trade volatility are not concerned about the price movement direction. Their target is to make a profit on increased volatility regardless of whether it rises or falls. You can use the Straddle strategy to take advantage of volatility in the market with the use of options.

Straddle Strategy with Options

The straddle strategy works well with options to trade volatility. Using options to trade volatility involves the trader buying a call option and a put option using the same strike price and expiration date. In this case, if there is a large price shift in the underlying instruments, both the call option and put option will be in-the-money for the trader and investor. Also, if the price rises, the call option brings in profits, and if the price falls, the put option brings money for the investor.

Take a look at the graph below:

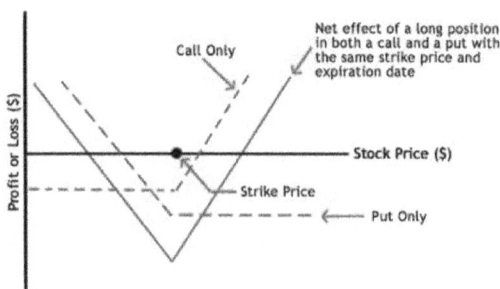

(mytradingskills.com)

In the graph above, an investor or trader can only lose if both the call and put options fail to yield. But if the price keeps moving away from the strike price in any of the directions, the investor enjoys profit. As we have mentioned from the beginning of this book that as much as there are risks associated with options trading, there are lots of profits attached to investing in it as long as you do it with the right knowledge. You can also trade volatility using the straddle strategy and pending orders. There is no doubt that your ability to trade volatility is needed for you to enjoy great profit from the options trading market. Knowing the way to do it and how to do it is the right information you need.

Chapter Four: Creating a Trading Plan

Planning is an essential factor we must all consider to be successful in life. If you fail to plan, you will act without direction, and this easily impedes success more than any other act. Every successful investor understands the need to plan out their investments to make profits. Planning your trading will give you the strength to be consistent and achieve your target. Many people don't take options trading seriously, and hence, they couldn't enjoy the benefits that come with trading options. Success in trading options doesn't come overnight. It requires proper planning and thorough homework.

Your options trading plan will outline the method you will adopt to trade, the amount you want to spend on the options, the level of risk you want to take, and you will have a measurement to know your overall performance. As a beginner, starting with a solid plan in mind will make you achieve success faster than you might have thought. As a trader, you've got to put all of yourself to execute your trade edge and, importantly, ensure you commit the plan to paper.

Why You Need a Plan

Emotion is a leading cause of failure in trading. Emotions can set in when you either make a profit or loss big. It gives your mind a certain spinning nature that may make you change your strategy and plans. But with a trading plan, you will be in check. Trading plans will present methodical instructions to you on how you can handle every situation that may arise during your trading. Also, you will have a guide on how you should handle multiple trades. Situations may get you anxious and lead to you losing out on certain opportunities, but with the help of your plans, you will know what to do at every point in time. Another benefit of setting up a trading plan is that it offers you the opportunity to know what will work and what won't work. If you are into random trading where you just buy and sell whatever options you see, it won't work for you effectively. But when you target the right options, and you monitor your progress, you will have an awesome result.

Preplanning Your Trading

Achieving success in options trading is not about creating a trading plan but about creating an effective plan. To do this, you've got to take some steps ahead of planning. You have to make some considerations and let them guide your choice. Let's take you through some things you've got to consider before you start planning.

Identify the best trading that works for your personality. There are various forms of trading, and all of these types work for different personalities. For example, if you are an active person, you can consider trading styles that involve daily activities, such as day trading or short-term trading.

Select the market you want to trade. You can choose among forex, stocks binary options, or any other security. If possible, you may combine. Just note that each of these markets has its pros and cons. But your plan will be based on your choice of market.

Identify your trading objectives. Know the reason you are trading. It is not enough to trade options just because you want to make more money. It may be that you want to make $100,000 in a year or buy a car. It may be that you want to make money to pay your kids' college tuition or anything. So, your trading plan should provide a means through which you want to achieve your objectives. Your objectives will always motivate you to persevere and keep trying, and at the same time, they will guide you on how best you can make trading decisions based on the available resources.

Creating Your Trading Plan

Every trading plan is personalized. The reason is that every trader thinks differently. Your trading plan will reflect your trading style, the level of your risk tolerance, and your preferences. This is why it is always advised that you take your time to set your trading plan yourself. You don't need the help of anyone. Just follow the basic components in this section and craft an awesome and result-driven plan for yourself.

Create Your Goals

Goals are needed to be the basis of your trading plan. Before you put your money into any trade or purchase that put or call options, ensure you have your goals analyzed and written out. Your goals should show your profit target. Make sure this is realistic. It will show the minimum risk you can take. What is the potential profit range for you to trade? There are traders who only trade when they see that the potential profit is twice or thrice greater than the risk in probability. Your goals can be weekly, monthly, or yearly. You've got to create time to re-assess them.

State your Risk Level

You've got to be intentional about this aspect of trading. Know the amount of your portfolio you can risk on a single trade. So, your risk tolerance level will determine this. The risk rate often varies depending on the trade, but ideally, it should only range between 1% and 5% of your portfolio every trading day. So, if you lose the amount you set in a day, you take a pause on trading for the day. A good way to trade is to know when to back down and re-strategize before you lose too much.

Do a Background Check

Traders are ardent learners and researchers. Before the market opens, ensure you read about the activities going on around the world. Know how the global market is faring. Know whether S&P 500 index futures are up or down in pre-market. This knowledge will help you gauge the mood of the market before the market opens because future contracts trade every time—day and night.

Be Prepared for Trade

Regardless of the trading system you are using, ensure you label minor and major support and resistance levels on the charts. Have your alert set for the entry and exit signals and set it in a way that you are sure you can see all signals or detect it with an audible auditory signal and clear visual signal.

Guide your entry point

Don't trade without setting entry rules. The entry rules should be simple that they will aid the possibility of making snap decisions. Set less subjective conditions when you set out to trade so that you won't find the whole process difficult. An entry rule could be:

If Signal X increases and there is the least target of nothing less than three times as high as my stop loss, I will buy Y contracts or shares here. You've got to be like a computer when it comes to abiding by your entry rules. Ensure that if the conditions you set are met, you make the move that follows. Don't be emotional about it.

Know when to exit by rules

Don't fall into the pit of seeking only the right signal of when to trade. Ensure you also pay attention to knowing the right time to exit. It is common among traders to find it hard to sell when they are down, all because they are afraid of losing. As a trader, who wants to be successful, learn to be strong and accept losses as they come because they are part of what makes trading work. What you need to do is identify your exit strategy right before you enter into a trade. Every trade gives at least two exits. The first is for you to know your stop loss if the trade doesn't go as you planned. Write down your stop loss, and don't just rely on your mental strength. Another exit strategy you should surely have is a profit target. Once you reach your profit target, sell a part of your position and move the stop loss over the other position up to the point of breakeven.

Record and Performance Analysis

Your plan should contain the system you want to adopt to record your trading activities. Your records should include listing the moments you had great wins, what you did right and how you did it. The same rules apply when you lose. Note why you lose and how. It will prevent you from making further mistakes along the line. Also, have a record of your target, and observe your entry rule and exit strategy. Your trading records should always be kept and saved for future analysis.

You have got to know that your effectiveness is not measured when you only keep records. The records are kept for a purpose—to check for future analysis of your performance. Know your loss or gains in the business, identify your mistakes and retrace them.

Being a success at options trading is a journey that you must be consistent on. You need to be resolute and make adequate preparation. Planning your trading activities will not only help you achieve success, but it will also make the whole process of trading easy and smooth. You will be able to monitor your progress and know where you need assistance. Planning ahead before trading will place you in a fast lane as an options trader.

Chapter Five: Adopting the Right Strategy

When people say that options trading is difficult and complex, they are not really lying. It is just that they fail to tell the truth about the need to understand the available strategies that can be adopted. There are several options trading strategies that you've got to know as a beginner who really wants to be successful in investing. Each of these strategies will give you the capacity to limit your risk and maximize your returns. Your knowledge of the right strategies to adopt will guide you and help you make informed decisions. It makes the whole process of investing easy and perfect. Let's take you through the strategies you need to know.

Covered Call

A covered call is a popular strategy used by many investors. It involves buying a naked option. Investors have the opportunity to buy-write or structure a covered call. This strategy is adopted by many investors because it helps to make more profits and has a low risk of staying longer on the stock alone. But note the trade-off behind this strategy. You have got to be willing to sell your security at a specific price, which is the short strike price.

Here is how the strategy works. Suppose you use a call option on a stock that is equivalent to 1000 shares of stock for every call option. If you buy 1000 shares, at the same time, you will sell one call option against it. It is called a covered call because it helps you if the price of the stock rises dramatically. Your short call will be covered by the long stock position. This strategy helps investors when they have a short-term position in a stock, and they don't have a definite opinion on how it is moving, So, they want to generate income by selling the call premium or by placing a protective measure around it in order to forestall a possible decline in the stock's value.

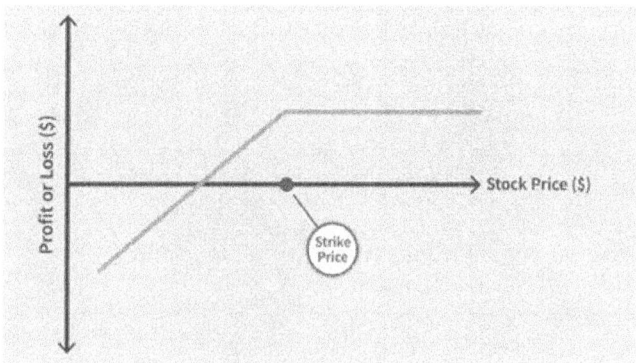

Covered Call Strategy

The covered call strategy graph above explains it clearly. As the price of the stock rises, the negative profit and loss that arise from the call are offset by the long share position. When the investor sells the call, the premium received gives the investor the opportunity to sell the stock at a higher rate than the strike price as the stock moves through the strike price to the upside. The result for the investor is the strike price and the premium received.

Married Put

For this strategy, you buy an asset, which may be a share, and at the same time place put options for the same number of shares. The holder of a put option can always sell the stock at the strike price. This strategy helps investors to protect their downside risk while they hold a stock. It helps to create a floor in case the price of the stock falls drastically. While this strategy helps an investor on the possible downside, it has a potential negative impact. If the value of the stock fails to fall, the investor will lose the premium paid for the put option.

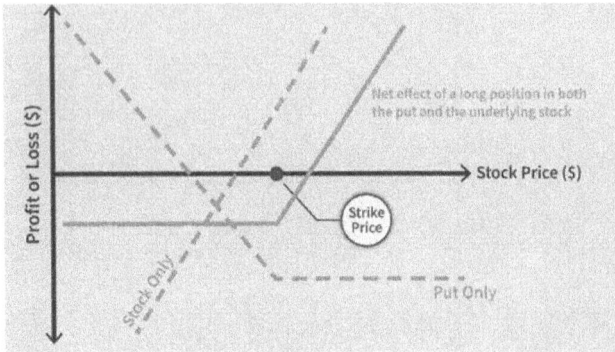

The Married Put Strategy

The graph shows the long stock position, which is represented by the dashed line. The long put and long stock positions are combined, and as the price of the stock falls, the losses are not high. But the stock is seen working in the upside more than the premium spent for the put.

Bull Call Spread

This strategy involves an investor buying calls at a given strike price and at the same time selling the calls at a much higher strike price. Investors use this strategy when they are sure that the price of the call will increase. The simultaneously sold call options will possess the same underlying asset and expiration date. With this strategy, you can easily reduce your upside on the trade and reduce the net premium you will spend. The Bull call strategy is a bullish strategy.

36

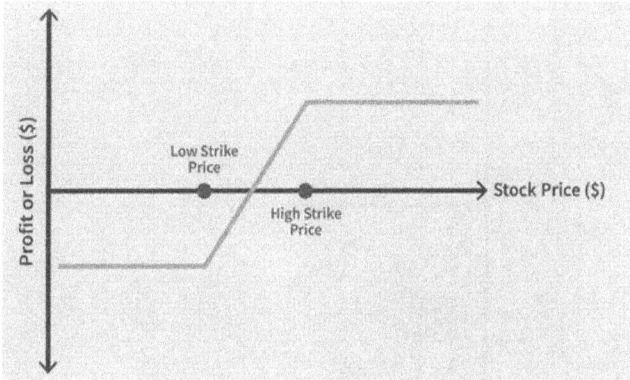

The Bull Call Spread Strategy

This graph explains how the strategy works. For you to be successful at using the strategy, you have to give room for the price of the stock to increase so you can make a profit when you trade. This strategy comes with a trade-off, and that is the fact that your upside is limited, despite the fact that the amount you spend on the premium is low. This strategy is set up in a way that when outright calls become high in price, you've got a way to offset the higher premium, which is for you to sell higher strike calls against them.

Bear Put Spread Strategy

This strategy is a form of vertical spread. It allows you to buy put options at a certain strike price, and you sell the put at a lower strike price simultaneously. Investors use this strategy when they have a bearish sentiment about the asset and have the opinion that the price of the asset will fall. With this strategy, the investor will experience both limited losses and limited gains.

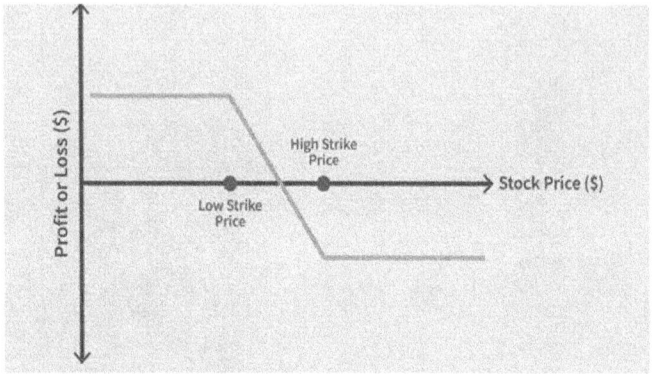

Bear Put Spread Strategy

The graph above explains the strategy. For you to be successful using this strategy, the underlying asset price must fall. This strategy makes your upside limited while your premium is also reduced. In a situation where the outright puts are expensive, you can sell lower strike puts against them to offset the high premium.

Protective Collar

This strategy involves buying an out-of-the-money put option and at the same time writing an out-of-the-money call option. For this trading, the underlying asset and the expiration are expected to be the same. Investors use this strategy when a long position in stock brings about substantial gains. So, with this strategy, the investor enjoys downside protection while the long put locks the possible sale price. However, the investor may have to sell shares at a higher price, which will likely lead to letting go of possible profits to be made in the future.

38

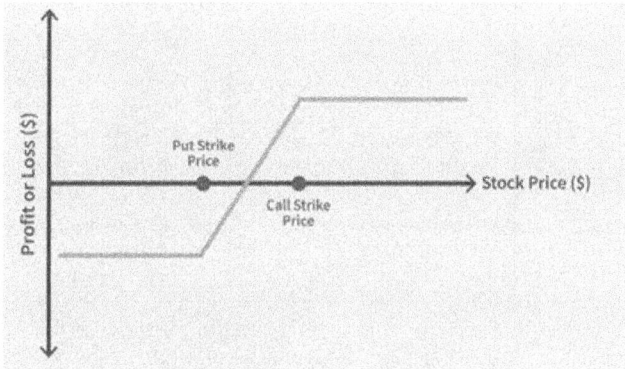

Protective Collar Strategy

In the above graph, you will see the protective collar. It is a combination of a covered call and a long put. This strategy protects the investor if there is a fall in the price of the stock, and while the investor may be forced to sell the long stock at the short call strike, there is a place of happiness in the sense that the investor already enjoyed gains in the shares.

Long Strangle

The long strangle strategy involves an investor buying an out-of-the-money call and put option that shares the same underlying asset and similar expiration date at the same time. A trader uses this strategy with the expectation that the underlying asset's price will grow; however, the trader doesn't know the exact direction it will take. The graph below explains it better. You will see two breakeven points. This strategy brings profits when the stock rises in either direction.

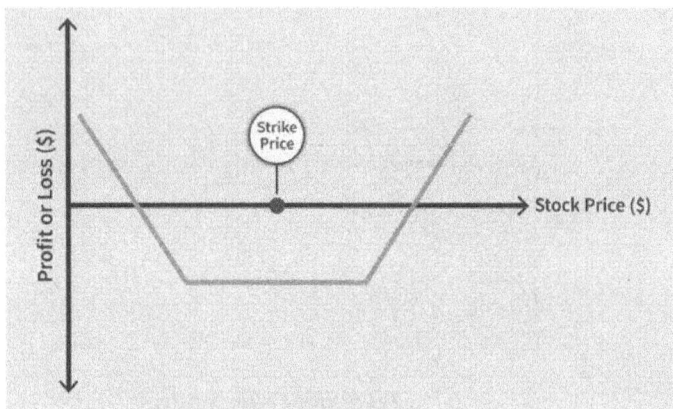

The Long Strangle Strategy

Long Call Butterfly Spread

This strategy involves the combination of a bull spread strategy and a bear spread strategy. It also involves the use of three different strike prices. The options are all for a single underlying asset and expiration date. A trader can buy a one-in-the-money call option at a low price and sell two in-the-money call options, and at the same time buy one out-of-the-money call option.

For the long call butterfly spread, the maximum gain is made when the stock doesn't change until expiration, which is the point of an at-the-money (ATM) strike. The longer the distance of the stock from the ATM strikes, the greater the negative change in the profit and loss of the trade. Note that the highest loss can occur only when the stock settles at the lower strike or below it. With this strategy, you will enjoy limited upside and downside.

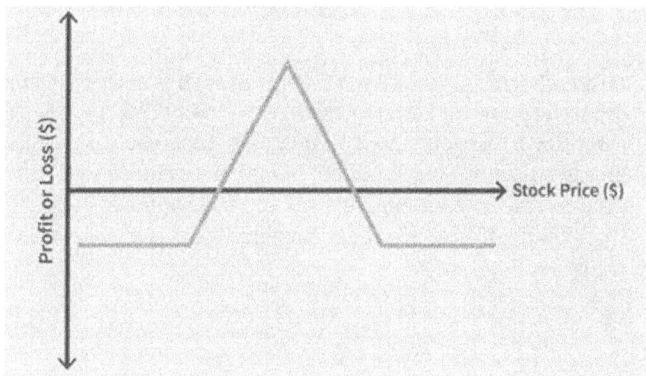

Long Call Butterfly Spread

Becoming a successful options trader involves consistent learning. The more you trade, the better you become at it, and the more you know, the better result you get. The strategies you can use to trade options are numerous, and you can keep learning more as you are immersed in trading. The key to becoming a better trader is to learn, do your research, and keep trading. As a beginner, your greatest fear should be to look for ways you can avoid mistakes as you trade. So, we have prepared basic information you need to prevent yourself from falling in your attempts. The next chapter will put you through how to avoid mistakes as you trade.

Chapter Six: Avoiding Trading Mistakes

Although it is necessary to gain enough knowledge about the different plans and strategies we have in options trading, it is also essential to understand the mistakes that you could face while investing within the market. Below are some errors that many options traders have experienced. In this chapter, we will talk about them in-depth, and show you how they can affect you as an options trader.

Lack of discipline

Many criteria fall under this. Different types of traders can lack discipline regardless of their knowledge level. You could be an experienced trader or an inexperienced trader that was taught by a very successful trader—who has taught you all you need to be a good trader and make money. Lack of discipline refers to traders who do not follow the rules and guidelines and prefer to take shortcuts to achieve bottom-line success; as I mentioned earlier, high win-rates do not signify an excellent trader. Ill-disciplined traders would be after getting a high win rate and would no doubt lack the courage to maximize profit yielding trades. Lack of discipline creates a fake aura of overconfidence and a phony sense of entitlement which would make them ignore their losses or look for ways to reduce them. The entitlement mentality would make them think they are overdue for a winning trade and make them forget money management principles. Such traders would pump money into a trade immediately after suffering losses in the hope of recovering their losses quickly, forgetting that the results of previous trades will not in any way affect the results of the next trade.

Wrong thinking about profit

The factors that help determine bottom-line profitability when buying options are win rate, average win, and average loss. All option buyers should aim for a win rate below 50% because you will be expected to pay a time premium that will reduce at a non-linear rate. You are also expected to make your market moves within a time frame; otherwise, you risk losing it because of its expiration date. The above factors make options trading less dependent on a high win rate as the main guarantee for profits is an average win rate that is higher than the average loss. This implies that you should maximize any opportunity for gains and always look for ways to reduce your losses if it is possible. High rates are misleading in options trading because it implies such traders are not effective in all opportunities and such kinds are prone to hold on losing trades, hoping it makes them become winners, which is a recipe for disaster.

Lack of diversification in your portfolio

Diversification in options trading applies to many aspects, from the strategies to plans, etc. Make it a priority to be aware of all the unknowns and how to react in different market environments. There are some strategies that apply to specific market conditions better than others, such as Straddles: A strategy that enables you to make significant gains from explosive moves in both directions without hindering the growth of your spreads. Also, there are other premium-selling strategies that bring in profits for you in an environment without directions. If you decide to use option trading as your only option, you can still make it as diverse as possible to maximize the gains that you can receive. Diversifying under an option buying strategy means you are exposed to both calls and puts them at different time frames. It gives you a setup for both call and put trades that can be used until your time is expired. A call set up could contain a break-out strategy that works based on momentum and a good strategy that searches for an oversold situation where the underlying is already going back to support.

Trading without an edge

Trading is a competitive journey that follows the standard rules of competitions. For example, the reason why tracks in relay races are staggered is to create a level playing field for all athletes. Imagine if the runner on the last lap that has the shortest distance in the center starts his or her race level with the first, it creates an advantage over others. This is what you should look for in options trading. What information do you have that others do not? What can you think of that most cannot? How can you turn privileged information into money-making opportunities or trades? You would only be able to maximize your chances if you have an edge that you can turn into a signal that can direct you on the possible movements of the market. Advantages in options trading involve getting hints about the direction of an underlying opportunity that the majority are oblivious to; or an open interest configuration; or the prices of many options that make the risk-reward attractive.

Misallocation of capital

There are many opportunities that would arise when you want to buy options. There are some that could present a chance to multiply your capital in many folds within a short time and make very significant gains. However, these opportunities could also cause you to lose all your capital if you choose the wrong option. So, when investing in high-risk trades that have the same possibilities for an increase or loss, make sure you do not commit all your funds to it. Leave more funds to trade with stocks than you commit to such trading options as it gives you a chance to maximize both opportunities. As a stock trader, you have the possibility to earn similar profits without undertaking excessive risks. Always give yourself the option to recover from losses and to not stake your entire portfolio on a short-term opportunity.

Poor option selection

There are many available directions that can be used by options traders. These include the numerous strike prices that are available with their time of expiration. Each available route has its own advantages and disadvantages. The benefit consists of the flexibility and capability to make your indicator work within the time frame where your move is expected to occur. A disadvantage is that availability of multiple options could be overwhelming for new and inexperienced traders. All traders can manage risks differently, and the type of options you will buy must go hand in hand with your risk tolerance ability. There are trades that offer more profits but come with the possibility of losing your entire investment. Such trades should be used with strike selection that will determine when the exercise price would become effective, especially when the trade is nearing expiration. The strike price and the time of expiration must be considered when selecting an option. The time frame must be aligned with indicators when trading options.

Mistakes are part of our life experiences. We grow with them if we are calculative enough. As a trader, your trading mistakes can either make or mar you. If you make the right mistakes, you will find yourself rising up and getting back on your feet. But the wrong mistake will stop you from ever trying to invest or trade again.

Conclusion

Options trading is a good way to build your wealth if done correctly. It offers you passive income that will help you achieve your financial goals. While many people believe that options trading is complex and difficult to achieve, successful, experienced investors and traders are making their money. We have provided you with the basic knowledge you need to build wealth around options trading. The information we have given will guide you as you make your debut, and as much as you learn and trade, you will become familiar with advanced and complex strategies you can use to become a pro as a trader. There is no better way to increase your money than to make it work for you. Learn the process now, and start making money as an options trader.

If you enjoyed this book in anyway, an honest review is always appreciated!

www.ingramcontent.com/pod-product-compliance
Lightning Source LLC
Chambersburg PA
CBHW031911200326
41597CB00012B/584